Totus Tuus

Totus Tuus

Clare M. Ashton

THE CHOIR PRESS

First published in 2007 by The Choir Press

Copyright © Clare M. Ashton

The right of Clare Ashton to be identified as the author of this work has been asserted in accordance with the Copyright, Designs and Patents Act 1988.

All rights reserved. No part of this publication may be reproduced or transmitted in any form or by any means, electronic or mechanical including photocopying, recording or any information storage or retrieval system, without prior permission in writing from the publisher.

ISBN 978-0-9535913-4-3

Produced by Action Publishing Technology Ltd, Gloucester
www.actiontechnology.co.uk

Contents

Abba Father	1
The Angry Chain	2
Alive!	4
Astounded	5
Babe of Bethlehem	6
The Beach	7
Castle Walls	8
Cost of Peace	9
Crown of Thorns	11
Dance in Your Laughter	12
Dreaming of Peace	13
Ebb and Flow	15
Eyes of Light	16
Father, Forgive Us	17
Friendship	18
Frozen Compassion	19
Gates to Heaven, Gates Of Hell	21
God's Refugee	23
Golgotha	24
If.....	26
Justice	27
Light Of Humanity	29
Light the Flame	30
Listening Ear	32
Love's Precious Fountain	33
On Eagle's Wings:-	34
One Day	35
Open Your Hearts	37

Peace and Regret	38
Peace In Our Time	39
Prince Of Peace	40
Pierced Cry of Peace	41
Powerful Pen	43
Praise of the Leper	45
Prepare	47
Promised Land	48
Questions, A Time for Healing	49
Quiet Man Of Galilee	52
Risen Conqueror	53
Rod and Staff	54
Presents or Presence?	55
Shadow of Your Wing	56
Singing Stars	57
Something's Gone Wrong Along The Way	58
Spiritual Insanity	59
Starry Night	61
Sunset	62
Take And Eat	63
Through The Sunshine	64
The Journey	65
The Wounded Face	67
Time	68
Totus Tuus	69
Trusting Broken	70
Voice of Angels	72
Where Did We Lose You?	74
Words and Silence	76
The Well at Calvary	79
Walk Beside Me:	81
Walking With Jesus	82

Abba Father

Abba Father, take my hands
And use them as your own
Abba Father, take my voice
I will praise You on Your Throne

Abba Father, I reach my hands
To your children who are in need
While selfish eyes and selfish hearts
Are focused on their greed

Abba Father, only you
Can cure their hunger and their thirst
Living God, Eternal, True
While greedy men do their worst

Hold the children rich or poor
Enfold them in your arms
In love or hate, in peace or war
And vanquish all their qualms

Loving Father, Spirit, Son
To slave and refugee
The Blessed God, the Holy One
The Holy Trinity

And on that Blessed, glorious day
When all our wars shall cease
We'll lift our eyes to heaven and say
"All hail the Prince of Peace"

The Angry Chain

Surrender and be
Surrender with me
Tender I shall be
And set your broken heart free

It's time to break the angry chain
Relish the sunshine, revelling in rain
Walking by the gently flowing stream
Give yourself the time to dream

Let go of anger and of rage
It's time to surrender, turn the page
Walk forward in faith once more
Surrender what has gone before

Leave your woes by Calvary's hill
Raging child, I love you still
And as you give yourself to me
The chains will drop, and you will see

That which you surrender, I return
In different form, and you will learn
The peace I give will set you free
The love I showed at Calvary

Sets free the hearts of angry men
Arising from the tomb once again
I reach to you, my child, and you will see
Love stronger than death has set you free

So surrender to my love once again
And see within the angry men
The pain and rage that they despise
Reflected in their broken eyes

And walk with me, your hand in mine
Speak My word and we will find
The hate and wounds that they bear
Their rage and pain, hatred, despair

Will vanish as the dawn appears
Through days and nights, months and years
Their hearts will return once more to me
And we will set the broken world free

To love

Alive!

Alive! that's what I want to be!
Able to laugh, to cry, to see
Able to run, to walk, to crawl,
And revel in the wonder of it all

So I wait in my mother's womb
To away, out of this living tomb
While I'm here I'm really growing
But I can't wait to begin knowing

Knowing what life is all about
To revel and dance, to sing and shout
To join in with games and enjoy my life
And know the meaning of trouble and strife

Please, oh please, give me a chance
To join in with life's merry dance
You'd consider setting killers free
If they can dance, then why not me?

Astounded

Your love sears through me
Astounded
I am left breathless
In the awe
That the aftershock brings

My heart reels
As it feels
The depth of love
Flooding from above
Its peace sets me free
I have liberty
From the past
And its chains

Your love tells me
This is the end
Of the search
The waypoint
And now
My journey starts
My companion
Of the heart
Beside me
From Calvary's tree
To set men free

And so we stride
No more to hide
Who I really am
For the Son of Man
Is by my side
And He will guide
Me home

Babe of Bethlehem

Can you hear rejoicing
Earth its praises voicing
For the babe of Bethlehem

Gaze at lowly manger
Where refugee and stranger
Met in strange embrace
In the gentle face
Precious babe of Bethlehem

Ox and ass adore Him
Kings kneel down before Him
Heav'n and earth before Him
Gentle babe of Bethlehem

Laid in lowly manger
No more foe or stranger
Kneel in wonder and in awe
Peace is present once more
Blessed babe of Bethlehem

Peace is given to humankind
Sight to those who are made blind
The key to life is seen
In the sight so keen
Tiny babe of Bethlehem

Turn once more, look again
Tired, old and yearning men
For the answer that you seek
Is written in the face so meek

Of the babe of Bethlehem

The Beach

Waves lapping gently on the shore
There, my restless heart will rage no more
For as it yearns, my soul it turns
To the peace I'm searching for

The waves treat the sand to a loving caress
I walk to greet the embracing peacefulness
A mind and heart free from troubles and strife
To enjoy the presence of God in my life

The joy I feel when I reach the one thing
The lyrics of the song I know how to sing
For I know that the beauty of the sea
Makes my life complete, my soul is free

I'm free to soar, soar like a dove
Dancing and singing in God's wondr'ous love
The love that so oft seems so out of reach
Until once more, I step onto the beach

Castle Walls

Castle walls so strong
Keep my heart safe, where it belongs
Yet when my soul yearns
My heart, it turns to see

The sails far to the east
Promising love, promising peace
Indecision taunts me, do I go, do I stay?

The captain beckons, well I know
The sunshine that melts a frozen heart's snow
So walking swiftly to the gate
Hoping wildly I'm not too late

Open the door, open your heart
Let the deepest healing start
Once more within those castle walls
Those deep and echoing halls

Laughter echoes once again
And the wounds made by bitter men
Are healed and soothed
My soul renewed and made whole

The castle with its walls so strong
Gives me comfort, yet I belong
Upon the ship with billowing sail
With captain sure, and direction true
I sail with love, my God to you

Cost of Peace

I seem so angry
Please tell me why
There seem so many
Tears to cry

There's nothing I feel
That warrants these tears
No sense of bitterness
And no hidden tears

And yet I feel so pained so sore
I feel sadness, and so much more
Where does it come from? Who can tell?
Feelings not mine, yet I know them so well

Words come unbidden, as I feel unshed tears
Unspoken words flow down the years
Cries for love, rejected before
Cries for peace, an end to war

What solution does it bring?
A strategy for an uncertain king?
And what of the bloodshed along the way
Those who never see another day

Yes as I gaze upon the world
It's pride and vanity boldly unfurled
Giving its youth as a sacrifice
Those naïve enough to pay the price

So, cry those tears of futility
Enough tears shed, maybe we'll see
That the answers we seek can never be found in war
The reasons lost in bloodshed and in gore

For as we fight, it's clear we've lost
With our lives we pay, too high a cost
Put down those guns, let the fighting cease
Let's cure this ill with words of peace.

Crown of Thorns

I see a crown of thorns
The blood runs down Your face
I behold a body torn
Yet I run from Your embrace

My hands, they long to take You down
And bathe Your hands, and feet, and side
Swamped in my own fears, I sink and drown
Submerged in my own pride

Yes, stubbornly, I keep my eyes
Averted from Your pain
But no memory can e'er erase
Those tears that fell like rain

Teach me, My Lord, I ask, I pray
To love the pain I see
For I know why I run away
I see Your pain in me

Dance in Your Laughter

I'll dance in your laughter
And drown in your tears
For when I'm beside you
I'll soothe all your fears

And when you feel lost child
As oft times you will
Just look for the answer
On Calvary's hill

Let the healing rivers flow
And touch the wounded, broken heart
Just reach out,
My child and know
We're never apart

For I am beside you all your days
In laughter and pain
And I will be in all your ways
The soothing gentle rain

The sunshine that warms you
The stars in the sky
And when the world's fears tire you
I'll sing a lullaby

So dance in the laughter
And sing in the rain
I am ever with you
To heal all your pain.

Dreaming of Peace

I stand, to face the east, to dream of love and dream of peace
To wait for the day when my soul is healed and the pain at last will cease
My heart is yearning for the day when like an eagle I will soar
Free from the chains of this world, free to weep no more

I start to turn away, to join the race of life once more
When suddenly someone starts to knock upon my heart's closed door
Should I turn the handle to let them in, or keep them out
My heart is filled with questions, and so much fear and doubt

While I'm thinking what to do and work out what's the score
I turn and notice something that I've never seen before
I see a steeply rising path up to a lonely hill
And it fills my soul with awe and wonder, I can see it still

There's something deep inside me saying this is the place I seek
There's solace for the lonely, downtrodden and the weak
For on that hill so lonely, so quiet and so still
A man was left to die, our sinfulness to kill

And so, drawn by the longing I feel within my heart
I turn the handle, open the door, the darkness falls apart
I see His Body battered, by a world so full of pain
And so I tell Him that in my heart, He can remain

I can't tell you I'm not scared, for that would not be fair
But I know deep in my heart, I have someone here who cares
And when I find myself lost in troubles that won't cease
I run into His loving arms to once more dream of peace

Ebb and Flow

The seas ebb and flow
Fear and love grow
In equal measure
Where is my treasure?

Fear enfolds me
Yet Your love holds me
In tension I see
Your love flows through me

One day I will see
How your love sets me free
But now I can only trust
Knowing I must
Hold tight
When fright
Overwhelms me

Hold my heart
When we're apart
I shed a tear
Lord hold me near

For you alone
Are my way
From night to day
So hold me fast
Knowing at last
The sun will rise
And in Your eyes
I will
Find peace

Eyes of Light

Come out of the darkness, and into the light
From sorrows and blindness, I'll be your sight
As you struggle and falter in the deep of the night
Walk out of the darkness and into the light

From a world full of muteness, to a life full of speech
From a tired world of weariness, to a peaceful, blest beach
To a deep sense of joy the world-bound cannot reach
Love and acceptance, with true joy I teach

I offer hope to the hopeless, and sight to the blind
Food for the hunger, deep within mankind
Soothing the hurt, and easing the mind
Helping those in deep sorrow, true joy to find

So come out of the darkness and into the day
For I am the true Light, the Life and the Way
When my love o'erfills you there's nothing to say
Come into My love and watch fear flee away

In the journey into day from deepest night
Your blindness and pain will melt in my Sight
Reach out to My light and you will see
The healing I give you has set your heart free

So go to the world, as it yearns for the light
Let them journey, with you, to day from deep night
Rejoice as their sorrow filled hearts are set free
And with newborn eyes of light you will see

Your God

Father, Forgive Us

For a world torn in two
An attitude of "I'm better than you"
For we know not what we do
Father, forgive us

For the hate of one another
For the fear of our own brother
Nation against nation, caught in the war
"We are all rich, there are no poor"
Father, forgive us

For our world and the state its in
For using our planet as a bin
For locking Christ out, not letting Him in
Father, forgive us

Forgive us for our hearts of stone
Turn them back to you alone
Please don't turn Your face away
To make our plight worse with each passing day

"Father, forgive us, we know not what we do"

Friendship

Friendship is a gift, a gift that can't be owned
It can't be lent or borrowed, or even merely loaned
It's giving and receiving, and learning not to take
It's trusting, undeceiving, so fragile it may break

It sees no divisions, no oceans, no continents
It sees only the friend, over distance small or immense
It reaches out in openness, it doesn't count the cosy
But make sure you guard it well, it can be easily lost

Life's journey can be tiring; it can be sore and can be cruel
You so quickly run out of dreams, your hope runs out of fuel
When we all have run the race, until the journey's end
Be thankful for the ones we loved and chose
To call our closest Friend

Frozen Compassion

O show us blessed Saviour
Where did compassion go
Was it buried in our anger
Lost in our frozen snow

Oh teach us loving Father
Not to betray your love
To hide the hand of your compassion
While wearing fear's tight glove

For you wish to cure cripples
And teach the lame to dance
To give the prisoner freedom
And with your love enhance

The lives of those who hunger
Give hope when in despair
The homeless cry to you Lord
Believing no-one cares

And yet you walk beside them
Your rod and staff and staff to guide
As they cry to you Lord
Your love is by their side

So teach us Lord to listen
And teach us Lord to care
As teardrops once more glisten
And hope turns to despair

For once the world was broken
And sin wandered wild and free
But the grip was finally broken
With lonely hill and tree

With your Son giving
Himself as sacrifice
We all Lord were owing
And yet He paid the price

So teach us Lord to reach out
To those who in their need
Can teach us once more
Ever once more
That you can heal our greed

Gates to Heaven, Gates Of Hell

The wind howls mournfully
As the gates rattle
People are no longer held here
Yet, there is need to remember

The wind cries
Remembering the slaughter
Of the innocent
Herod's deeds
Reflected in the chambers

They suffered, yet bore it humbly
God suffered with them, every one
Those helpless ones, led to the slaughter
In the hell created by one

Who stripped himself of all emotion
Stripped himself, stripped so bare
For how else could he, with devotion
Condemn to death all who were there?

For as he turned from his humanity
And the veil from him was torn
It paved the way to the insanity
And many were then left to mourn

The gates once more are closed
The task they did is done
In it's role as mighty sheepfold
Innocents slaughtered, one by one

Listen, hear now the wind's mournful cry
And remember, if you will
The echoes of that lullaby
Murmured first on Calvary's hill

For cries of pain and cries of sorrow
Old ones, new ones, uttered still
Whether in a camp in Auschwitz
Or upon a lonely hill

So take heed, and learn a lesson
Learn it quickly, learn it well
When we see humanity forgotten
We can see a living hell

When we want to feed our pride
And forget our fellow man
When humanity is denied
It is right that we demand

Never again the gates be opened
Let them remain shuttered tight
And let us guard those gates closely
Let not in the dark of night

And when the wind calls and cries a lonely
Reminder of what went before
Let it say to us only
Prevent it now, and evermore

For when you ask where was the Father
On those dark and fateful days
He walked into those darkened chambers
And into that deepening haze

For yes, He wept, as those He cherished
Herded, derided, walked to death
Cried in anguish as they perished
Taking their final breath

For they were all God's children too
Family, brethren, cousins, kin
The family of God, they knew
And into Heaven entered in

God's Refugee

My refuge and my rock
One true source of peace
When pain and sorrow rock
My heart I find release

In a love that cannot be measured
A price that cannot be paid
A value far more to be treasured
Than silver or gold inlaid

The love of God surrounds me
Enthralls me, and astounds me
Lost in wonder and awe
I gaze, lost once more
In the peace and joy I know can set me free

So once again I gaze
At the Ancient of Days
Whose love has set me free
My loving Father, He renews my soul

Golgotha

One Friday morn a Father was crying
His Son hung on a cross painfully dying
The Jews taunted loudly, for all men to hear
Behind all their teasing was deep pain and fear

Fear of what they might actually have done
Was that man hanging there really God's Son
Was this the Messiah, by prophets foretold
And why did the morning seem so bitter and cold?

If this man dying, so human He seemed
was really God's Son, would they all be redeemed
And if they had killed Him, then what would they do
For Yawheh's heart would be broken in two

If this man's teaching was to believed
Then all was not lost, and could be retrieved
Yes, if that was so, what that man had said
Well, let's leave it and see, was what many said

All He'd predicted so far had come true
They found it all so uncanny, don't you?
There were some strange things happened that day
the Temple curtain being torn that way

He'd been rather quiet, that man hanging there
You'd think He'd show anger, or even despair
And though nearly two thousand years have gone by
The world will remember that dying man's cry

Yes, my friend, He's still hanging there
For He is the Light in this world's despair
Look toward the man hung on Golgotha's hill
You'll find your soul healed, if only you will

For although it's there, the cross isn't the end
It's the start of a brand new life, my friend
If you can accept that man, so battered and so torn,
In the love of the Risen Christ you will be reborn!

If.....

If the world were one big jigsaw, which piece would you be?
If the world were one large body, I know I'd be the knee
If the world were a chocolate cake, would we all eat?
Would it be our first good meal, or yet another treat?

If the world just stopped revolving, would we fly off into space?
And all be free-fall astronauts, the entire human race?
If people could look beyond the curtains that veil our inner eyes
And listen to the one who can soothe our aching sighs

If masks could be transparent, would you really want to see?
The person that you're used to, or the child that's really me?
If the world wasn't so tattered, so broken and so torn
Maybe we'd see the beauty of each brand new glorious morn

If people could slow down, what a landscape they would see
With a portrait of the one who set all of mankind free
Compassion in His features, and love within His eyes
With the One who truly loves us, there is no more disguise

Yes, if the heart was quietened and if our lives were still
If we took the old and winding road, up to that lonely hill
If by taking chances, to the Father we could yield
We'll look into our soul's mirror, to one day find we're healed

Justice

Justice won't be found between the pages
While all the time the battle rages
With brother intent on killing each other
For the fear of losing to one another

Yes, idleness is no good
and apathy won't stop shedding innocent blood
We can all pray for an end to the killing
and ask fervently for peace, God willing

It's amazing what a war
Is supposed to be good for
There wasn't so much petty crime
When we had a war from time to time

Yes, and people weren't out of work
Excepting you were an idle jerk
A good-for-nothing or so they'll say
Another statistic to be hidden away

What a load of feeble excuses
Money could be put to better uses
Instead of fighting our own fear
and musing into our pints of beer

Justice screams to you each day
but our fear gets in the way
telling you not to get involved
And that someday the problem will be solved

We can't afford to just sit back
and hope that someone has the knack
To make these problems go away
As they get worse each passing day

Yes, justice stares us in the eye
We hear it in Christ's dying cry
And truth is such a dirty word
Don't try too hard, it might get heard, BY YOU!

Light Of Humanity

Light of sanity
In our humanity
The peace in our life
Throughout moments of strife

The sense of belonging
Overcoming the longing
The yearning inside
For somewhere to hide

The salt of this world
Your banners unfurled
The city built upon a hill
With Your love, our empty lives fill

Your arms open wide
The friendship inside
Saying, "I love you so,
My child, don't let go"

Yes, light of humanity
In the dark of pain
You are our sunshine, Lord
After the rain

Light the Flame

Lord light the flame
Dispel the night
Show the light
To the children who yearn

Light the hearts
Yearning in darkness below
To their brokenness show
The beauty of your love

Let the fire burn
As the wounded turn
Their broken hearts
Once more to you

Let the fire burn
And the world rejoice
Once more to hear
The beauty of your voice

Talk once again to your world
The work of your mighty hands
Reach down and touch the wounded ones
That they may know your peace

For your pow'r has no end
Your love sets us free
And we truly can be
Part of your loved
Part of your world
Part of the beauty of your world

Part of that wonderful world
Part of the power you unfurled
Power that sets us free
Power that lets us be

Yours alone

Listening Ear

When you listen do you hear
The voice that is so near?
Watch the lantern, see the light
That dispels the deepest night
If you follow you'll find the way
From the night into the day

Do you revel in the rain
Without overwhelming pain
Do you give your feelings voice
And your heart time to rejoice?

Do you find the time, and seek the key
To truly once more be set free
For the laughter of the child
Is the love of God so mild

Use your eyes and you will see
There is love and liberty
Use your heart and soul again
Join the song of peaceful men

Hear the chorus of the song
Of the ones we know belong
To the choir of the ones
He called to know they belong

So open your ears and open your heart
And together once more we'll start
To love the ones despised by men
And teach them all once again

To sing

Love's Precious Fountain

There's a quietness I seek in the cleft of a mountain
Where the stream trickles into love's precious fountain
where the fields are verdant and I know,
that streams of living water flow

I walk along the peaceful shore
Somehow my heart aches no more
As I hear the Spirit's gentle call
And I see the beauty of the waterfall

I walk now to the edge of a cliff
The breeze is loving and gentle, never ruffling, never stiff
The water plumes in a radiant cascade
To settle in a sleepy glade

I find myself in a darkened cave
There's freedom here, I am no slave
The light I see is His love revealed
And I see, once more, I have been healed

So once more refreshed I return to the fray
Having seen the break of day
I shall not fear even the deepest night
For He is the Way, the Truth and the Light

On Eagle's Wings:-

On eagle's wings you shall surely fly
Tirelessly, freely, across a clear blue sky
With the strength of the Lord, never to fall
The Lord you God hears your joyful call

So fly, my child, so strong and free
Fulfil your each and every dream
The gentle breeze to guide you on your way
And the love of the Father to brighten the day

The air smells so fresh, and life seems so sweet
With the Lord your God, every day is a treat
The Lord your God knows your ev'ry need
And with His love you are free indeed

And when, at last, you seek to land
The rock of the Lord is close at hand
The journey over, the work complete
You may sleep securely at Christ's pierced feet

One Day

One day as I listened
The Lord beckoned, "Follow"
And once more I found
The world seemed so hollow

The lights of the city
So familiar to me
Looked once more like baubles
Sparkling on a tree

And all of my life here
The things done so far
Were only a glimpse Lord
Of what we truly are

Look at these friends Lord
Children of God
It is quite amazing
The steps that we trod

Were trod long ago Lord
When you moved on this earth
And gave all mankind
A chance for new birth

The time it is hastening
It's time to move on
And I hear your call Lord
It's time to be gone

To be with my Saviour
My Lord and My Friend
He was my beginning
My life and my end

And when I meet you Lord
As we do face to face
I am so looking forward
To that loving embrace

For deep in your love Lord
I stand by your side
Across Jordan's deep river
And it's divide

For when you gave your life Lord
To set us all free
It meant that my death Lord
Is the beginning for me

And as we look down Lord
At the world far below
I know in my heart
That my love now will grow

So I move forward boldly
And walk in your grace
Knowing I'll be caught
In your loving embrace

Open Your Hearts

Open your heart to me
As I am on Calvary's tree
Open your hearts to me

My love is given free
To all who need
All I ask you to be
Is open to Me

Let your tears fall like rain
Let my love soothe your pain
Let my peace heal your soul
Soothe you, make you whole

Let my grace wash away your sin
Soothe that ache deep within
The one that won't let you be
Open your heart to me
And I'll set you free
Oh open your heart to me

And open your soul

Peace and Regret

Don't you feel it's time to put down the sword?
To take the time and listen to my word?
Can't you see it's time to let go of the gun?
Can't you tell when the race is run?

You say you want the ache to cease
You say your tired hearts yearn for peace?
Why then, can you explain to me
That rifle is held with such glee

The chains that bind are your own regret
The anguish and torture, the sorrow you let
Those hands, so wounded, so broken and torn
Will unlock a soul yearning to be reborn

So reach out those hands, place them in mine
See in the bread and in the wine
The prison, the prisoner, captive and free
are all in plain sight, it's you and it's me

Peace In Our Time

Peace in our time, peace of mind,
you'll be lucky if you find
Peace in our time, peace at all,
will you hear the silent call of peace?

Peace is crying silent tears
Seeing all our deepest fears
Feeling all our deepest pain
How long will those tears remain in our hearts?

When will wake up and see
The price He paid to set us free
For until we accept His gentle release
It's sad to say, but there'll never be peace in our time

How can we have peace in our time
If we all don't cease this endless mime
Rejecting all the love in me
Denies the chance to set others free from pain

Open up, if you feel you can
To welcome in a peaceful man
Look into a wounded face
And lose yourself in an embrace of peace

Prince Of Peace

Prince of Peace, Son of God
War dwells in the land you trod
Your chosen people, torn apart,
A peaceful man, it breaks Your heart

Why, oh, why, can we not learn
You have the peace for which we yearn
We turn our backs and walk away
Facing our conflict for one more day

The peace of God is what we desire
Your flame of peace sets us on fire
With love for a God whom we cannot see
And for His Son who sets us all free

Show us lord, your waters are calm
Your voice is so gentle, your presence so balm
Lead us out of this eternal strife
And show us the special things in life

And maybe, just maybe, we will see
The peace which we seek can set us all free
On that happy day, all fighting will cease
And your Kingdom on earth will be a kingdom of peace

Pierced Cry of Peace

The gull's piercing cry
The crystal blue sky
The sea and the shore
Creator adore

The glorious crashing waves
Sing to Him who saves
Enthroned in majesty
Once again we see

Mountains mightily soar
Seas and oceans roar
Their voices gladly praise
Our God, the Ancient of days

The one whose feet strode
The universe when time began
Who cared and loved into life
Every woman, every man

Gentile, Jew, rich or poor
Strangers no longer,
Lone pilgrims no more
Lending voices to the chorus
The song written long before

Before the world became so broken
Before its beauty was so torn
Words of anger yet to be spoken
In the light of a new morn

Find your hearts and find your voices
Search out the love you have inside
When you face life's many choices
Let the Holy Spirit guide

Open your heart, and let your love flow
Reveal your soul to the father above
For as you do, His love inside you will grow
Your life sealed with the sign of his love

And as His love grows, it will flow, oh, so freely
And flowing, and growing, His peace will endure
In the lives of His faithful, His presence is showing
On the world He created His love will outpour

On a world who is battered, and a child who is torn
For in the night of despair,
our God's love is a beacon
Leading us gently towards the new morn

He leads us, so gently, tenderly carried
Towards the dawning of His love's new day
The ones in the world, who are endlessly harried
The sheep and the lambs who have gone astray

The love of our father gently enthrals us
The total acceptance in Christ's eyes
As once again the Spirit inside calls us
To listen again to the gull's piercing cries

Powerful Pen

Don't ask me
Where they start
Those crazy words
Forming a part

Of a poem on a page
Players on a stage
Where the author with a pen
Writes the lives of broken men

As the flow, the way they pour
Can make a broken soul soar
Can make a wounded bird take wing
Can give a silence a song to sing

The pen can give such souls release
As they strain once more for peace
And as the writer scribbles down
The feelings that can make them frown

The fears, the joys, regrets and more
The testimony to bitter war
The futile grasp of sword and shield
Temptation to regret to yield

For expression breaks the evil spell
Of the wounded soldier's hell
And gives them strength to carry on
When many others have long gone

And reach out for that distant shore
Where love and peace stand at the door
Where fear and hate forever banned
Are strangers in that sacred land

And if the words that flow again
Can soothe the souls of bitter men
Then once again I see their touch
Can for so many mean so much

So when those words flow to the pen
And give the writer once again
The need to place them on the screen
The love they have will often mean

A chance to live

Praise of the Leper

He sits with the leper
He walks with the lame
And our hearts are resounding
In praise of His Name

In awe as those
Sitting by Galilee
We are entranced Lord
Simply to be

Gazing at your face
The world could not replace
The love so freely given
By the one truly risen

And so Lord we walk
Along paths that seem so long
Sometimes we can even talk
Sometimes we're not that strong

So hear us, our Father
When the words will not find a way
Of opening our hearts
To show your love today

In a world that is broken
A world that is so torn
When dark words are spoken
Show us the light of the morn

And when the night
Yields unto the day
We will see Your light
Your truth, Your way

And children of God
Young and old, Gentile and Jew
Tread the path so many trod
In the journey unto You

And when at last
We find journey's end
We greet our Saviour
And our friend

Prepare

Prepare
Be aware
Take care
For the Lord is coming soon

Be on guard
For it is hard
No holds are barred
For He is coming
soon

The Baptist's cry
Announcing
the Lord passing by
For He is coming
soon

Make straight the way
The valleys fill
And flatten down
The mighty hill

Yes prepare the way
For the day
When He arrives
For He is coming
Soon

Promised Land

Why are you so wild,
my hurt and broken child?
Do you seek a place to hide,
slip into my wounded side

Do you need a place to stay
A resting place along the way
A chance to be once more inspired
Refreshed anew instead of tired

Tired of running from this pain
Wanting sun instead of rain
Wanting joy instead of fear
I will speak what you want to hear

The world is greedy, weak and cruel
It delights in making you a fool
Taking a perverse delight
In flirting with an endless light

But, my child, you don't belong
In this world where pain's so strong
You, my child belong with Me
Peaceful, joyful, rested free

Reach out those weary arms once more
And strike out for a distant shore
When you reach the promised Land
I'll be there, reach out your hand
To me…

Questions, A Time for Healing

Why
Do we go on?
When long gone
Is the reason
To trust?

And why
Do you lie
When all I
Wanted
Was to
Trust?

Are friends
Always doomed
To wound
Each other?
Or can
Humanity
Truly love?

Maybe
The answers
Are there
Staring us in
Our face
A place
We don't
Always
Look

And maybe
It's worth
The risk
To reach out
And love
Another
Selflessly

And given time
The wounds of mine
So recently made
Will slowly
Heal once again

So I will
Withdraw
Take time
Once more
And pull
The door
To my heart
Closed
To all except
Those
Who I can truly
Count friends

And someday
Not to far
When my scar
Has faded
I will once more
Reach out
And open this door
And let others
In again

But you and I
Lord will try
And by and by
The world and I
Might make
Some form
Of bond

Just understand
When you hold my hand
That I want you near
But the real fear
That lives inside
Will always hide
Who I can be
When you're with me

So, please take heart
That a start
Has been made
And the blade
That wounds me so
Did not go
Too deep

To trust again
May mean
I will have to open
And so I slide
Into my shell
So I can
Once more
Repair

Quiet Man Of Galilee

A quiet man to set us free
The quiet man from Galilee
A revolution about to start
A revolution in our hearts

A spark burst swiftly into flame
Wills surrendered to His Name
The light of God providing life
Dispelling darkness, death and strife

Did you hear his screams on the day He died?
Did you feel His anguish as He cried?
As He found His voice and set us free
That quiet man from Galilee.

Risen Conqueror

Oh my sweet Redeemer King
To you my praises I will bring
Your glorious story I will tell
Of your victory over Hell

Our salvation now assured
By you our conquering Lord
Destroying death's most final power
The triumph of the lily flower

The screams of rage as Satan fled
Once more to Hell, with fear and dread
The power for so long that held sway
Crumbled in the light of Easter Day

The missing stone, the empty tomb
The shafts of light that pierced the gloom
So wipe away your frightened tear
For liberation day is here

Rod and Staff

As we walk with the light you show us
Ever onwards will we journey
Through the darkness
Into a brand new day

Rod and staff have I
With you ever nigh
They comfort me once again
When faced with bitter men

Hearts of stone turn into flesh
When your love touches their soul
Fear and anger flee
When our dignity
Roars again

For children of God are we
His love gives dignity
Hope to all

Whether slave or free, old and young alike
None are worthless, all are loved
Grant us wisdom lord, may our leader's sword
Yield to words of peace

As our days go by
Sing a lullaby
Rod and staff us comfort still
As you reveal your will

To our world

Presents or Presence?

Can you hear the angels singing?
Or is it simply cash tills ringing?
The crib, and manger, ox and ass
Are lost in our greed, harsh and crass

Did good Santa in his sleigh
Take Christ's message far away?
As he raced to give his gift?
Did he the true message lift?

Sparkling lights, full shopping malls
Drowning out the angels calls
And lost for yet another year
The message Christ Our Lord is here

He's in the sellers in the street
Big Issue vendors, who will meet
Stressed out shoppers as they race
Past nameless figures, showing His face

Shops are heaving, plenty there
They once again leave manger bare
As humankind have their way
To celebrate the Saviour's birthday

Would you go to a party, go to a feast?
Where the first are last and the rich are least
Where invitation depends not on a full purse
And men are blessed, none better, none worse

So pause in your feasting as we rejoice
At the birth of a babe who's quiet, still voice
Resounds in the mall at the close of day
And reminds us all that Christmas Day

Is for peace

Shadow of Your Wing

Nestling in the shadow of your wing
Brings me Your peace
And I long
Once more to be at your side
Watching your children's pride
Destroy the world your hand has made

I long once more to seek your face
For no earthly friend will ever replace
The yearning in my heart to be with you
Faithful One, my Father true

So I shelter in your loving arms
Knowing the world, with all it's charms
Will never satisfy the need in me
Knowing that Your peace will set me free

To walk once more with broken men
Seeing the light of Christ once again
As I journey with fellow pilgrims on my way
Through the darkness to light of blessed day

Pilgrims on the road, we toil
Eking rest on unforgiving soil
Yet I know, as we go
You will teach us and will show

Your way

Singing Stars

As the stars proclaim your glory
And the skies shout forth your praise
As they tell creation's story
You stride the skies, Ancient of Days

Ever watchful and all knowing
Mindful of Your own Creation
Setting stars above e'er glowing
And starting out on our salvation

Forging promises with our forebears
Teaching them to hope and pray
Pointing onward, making them aware
Of the coming Easter Day

Loving, guiding, and preparing
Humankind for that great day
When Your Son, human form wearing
Swept the power of sin away

Swept along a mighty river
Ever part of that great flood
Forgetting all the sin of ages
Washed away by His Precious blood

The heavens sing the wondrous story
They sing your praise, Ancient of Days
It's time to proclaim your Endless glory
Lost in wonder, awe and praise

Something's Gone Wrong Along The Way

Whatever happened to love one another
When brother won't even talk to brother
And the rest of the world thinks it's O.K?
Nations rising up for war, makes me wonder even more
If something's gone wrong along the way

How can we watch other's pain, and apathetic still remain
When we believe in Jesus Christ, or so we say?
How can we sit back and see the humiliation of poverty,
Yes, something's gone wrong along the way

Did Christ die for the privileged few,
or is His gospel really true
That the poor will claim the Kingdom one day?
And what are we all going to do when he asks,
"Well who are you,"
and "Did you spread the Gospel in the right way?"

"And what about the unborn child,
who cried out to me, so meek and mild,
When its precious gift of life was snatched away?
Why do people ignore me when I died and rose to set them free
Oh, something's gone wrong along the way

Forgive us for our hearts of stone, turn them back to you alone
And help is all to see the light of day
Maybe when we turn back to you,
then we can decide just what to do because
Something's gone wrong along the way!

Spiritual Insanity

When you're losing your sanity
In this mess called humanity
When you struggle and fight
In this world's angry night

Stop the thrashing, cease your rage
There's chaos enough on this broken stage
Take the time to ease your heart
Watch your dreams before they fall apart

Gather your ideas, guard them well
Before you know it, they'll tumble and you'll watch where they fell
What's happened, bemused you ask,
too scared to take the world to task

Go on, let go, stand aside, walk away
Don't fight the night or give in to despair
Look at the man who gave and came to dare
He dared to give His heart for you

He dared to open His arms and die for you
Can you hear the anguish in the cry that He made for you?
He's there, O my Lord, He's there,
Just look at His love, see it in His dying stare

Love the pain that you see in those eyes
That's God's love in there, there's no disguise
Reach out to Him as He gives His all for you
His love has no limits, it will pull you through

It will give you new courage,
your soul will take to the wing
Love Him again,
join the song His children can sing

Starry Night

Starry night, gently keeping
guard over a world that is sleeping
Makes me feel the restful way
That life prepares for the next day

Majesty of a God of Love
Echoed in the stars above
If you're lucky, you'll see Mars
Or Venus playing with the stars

Yes, the night makes me feel small
the view of stars leaves me enthralled
Thinking how lucky I must be
For the God that made them, He loves me!

Sunset

The sun descends on another day
Close your eyes, it'll be okay
The clouds above being lit with sleep
the Lord will his watchful eye ever keep

So trust in His love, my child tonight
And slumber till the morning light
The worries of another day
Will never seem so far away

The evening now closes its eyes
The moonlight touches you with its sighs
The Lord your God is by your side
And in His loving embrace, you can hide

And when you awake, refreshed you will be
To once more set the people free
Who during the day fuss and fight
And fear the sunset and night

Take And Eat

Tonight, we are together, and I am by your side
My heart is close to breaking, and these tears are hard to hide
The dawning of a new day, my death will surely bring
As the fear of a nation puts a crown of thorns upon its chosen King

My time on earth nigh over, my mission nearly complete
But one last thing I ask of you, please take and eat
My body bruised and broken, so battered and so torn
For my dying offers you a chance to die to sin and be reborn

This cup of wine before me now, will be my very blood
Take it now and drink it, for it represents some good
Some goodness in a world that is so evil and depraved
And out of the next dark day to come, many souls will be saved

So please remember my request for you to take and eat
My body and my blood whenever you will meet
I will surely rise again, just as the prophets foretold
And come to give you guidance, in days that are so cold

And when I leave you once again, to take my rightful place
At the right hand of my Father's throne, the throne of grace
I will be among you whenever you will meet
To praise the One who asked you to simply "take and eat"

Through The Sunshine

Through the sunshine through the laughter and the pain
Through the night and through the day
Stones that bar the path and block the way
Through the clouds of the tears
And the journey of the years

There's an echo deep inside
Resounding where I choose to hide
A heart that beats in time with mine
Telling of love divine

Walk again, walk in peace
Let the raging inside cease
Let the candle of love light the way
As we come into the day

Leaving doubt and fear behind
In the caverns of your mind
Watch the light diffuse the fear
As I touch your heart, you'll find me near

The Journey

When did You choose me,
When did it start?
When did you first knock
Upon the door of my heart?

When did You whisper?
Those words of Your love?
Showing Me your path?
Father above?

When did Your Spirit
First open my heart?
When did my love for You
Make a start?

I can't really answer
I don't really know
Of the love deep inside me
Watching me grow

Watching me falter,
Watching me fall
Watching me stumble
Hearing me call

One thing I remember
Is the outstretched hand
Guiding me safely
Onto solid land

Away from the turmoil
So deep in this soul
Onto the land's firm soul
Making me whole

So does it matter?
When the journey began
For I know my companion
Is the Son of Man

The Wounded Face

When you're weary and oh, so alone,
When there's no-one left to turn to
and the crowd has all gone home
It's so easy to despair, when you feel that there's no-one there
And the hearts that are left are made of stone

Yes the emptiness of a broken heart
has a message written there
It asks for a chance to love, a chance to really care
But the love that's inside has so oft been denied
That your soul wonders if there's any there

You feel so abandoned, so lost and so confused
The world has picked you off life's fruitful tree
and you've been kicked and bruised
But there is a way for you to use the love so true
That is locked away so deep inside you

His face may well be battered, His Body surely torn
But His Love death has shattered, that you might be reborn
That instead of fear, the voice that you hear
Is offering the chance to see a new morn

Yes, the Lord may not look pretty unto the worldly eye
And many people run away from His dying cry
But His love beyond compare is a fact that is ever there
So lose yourself to Him, to a selfish world die

Time

It is time
Child of mine
That you are set truly free
To be
Alive

And the wounds
That you bear
From other's rage
And despair
Will heal
With the dawn
Of a brand new morn

Look at Me
I set you free
Calvary's tree
Is just the beginning
The winning
Of life over death
My last breath
A triumphant cry

For you see
We are both free
Death where is the victory
Where is the vicious sting
When we are with
The glorious King
Of life?

Totus Tuus

When the world tries to subdue us
Holy Spirit, renew us
Dear Father, near to us
Always stay close

When the waves overwhelm me
When the dark nights condemn me
When the loneliness haunts me
When the bitterness taunts me

Then Your hand reaches to me
Fear no longer subdues me
Emboldened anew
I reach out to You

For many things I can stand
With the touch of Your hand
In my own

And the world
Attractive tho' it be
Holds no attraction
For me

Teach me to reach out
Take away fear and doubt
Once more, Lord renew us
Let us be totus tuus
Once more

In memory of Pope John Paul II

Trusting Broken

Of what am I so afraid?
Of the promises that are made
Of the words so softly spoken,
and the heart once more is broken

You say to trust in You,
I honestly want to
But every time I do,
I lose my heart to you

So these words aren't meant to hurt?
Why doesn't that ring true?
I've been too often burnt,
to readily trust you

But as I journey on,
the reasons seem all gone
No more a need to fear,
when peace and love are near

So help me lose these chains,
they are all that remains
Of the wounded angry one,
who met Your wounded Son

And take this rage away,
to help me find my way
And climb back to the Son,
to find the battle won

For maybe I will find,
love and the peace of mind
For which my hurt soul yearns,
as to You it turns

So teach me Risen Lord,
Once more to seek your word
As once more it seems I must,
reach out to you and trust

And maybe then that fear,
will one day disappear
And with joy be replaced,
as I gaze upon your face

Voice of Angels

Can you hear the angel voice
As the heavens rejoice
As they sing
Voices ring
Hosannas bring
To a silent earth

Ox and ass
Stand quietly by
Mary sings
A lullaby
To the babe
Who brings us peace
The wars will cease
When He reigns

O reign in power
One of might
Whose hand stars and sea
Brought to birth
Made the earth
You walked
As man

O mystery divine
That saviour mine
Could come to me
And set me free

When with His death
His saving breath
Set us free
Once more to be

Amazed again
Astounded men
In fields with their sheep
Gaze in awe
Once more

Babe in the manger
Nestling in the hay
Shows the way
To Father dear
Who ever near
Freely shares

His peace

Where Did We Lose You?

Oh where did we lose You
Where did you go?
Was it us that left You
Or did you truly know

That we would turn away once more
Searching in vain for what we lost
Not looking at the price you paid
Not counting the cost

Seeing our loneliness and our fear
Looking in other places,
Denying you're near

And when we are weary
As oftimes we'll be
Oh Lord, our answer
is found at Calvary's tree

The lights are so gaudy
they attract our eye
and yet they are shallow
and don't satisfy

The heart that is searching
The aching that's there
for deep in those streets Lord
They still have that despair

For silence speaks deeper than many a word
And once again the voice is heard
One that we must strain to hear
That promises life free from fear

So, reach out, grab hold, and walk with me
To the silent hill, and the lonely tree
The tears cried there cleanse both heart and soul
And once again you will be whole

Teach us, O Lord, when we feel so lost
When the world and it's pain wreaks the cost
For a heart shattered with loss and fear
Can be healed when You are near

So, still our lives, and soothe our heart
And show us once more, we are a part
Of the world so lovingly made
And so freely, and proudly displayed

And when you gaze upon your child
Who can be angry, lonely, wild
Remind them that your love is always there
To soothe their wounds, and ease their despair

Words and Silence

I hear you talking
As I am walking
Are my ears deceiving
Me into believing
That silence alone
Is present here?

So as I journey
You're by my side
My rod and staff
Comforter and guide

And when I falter
When I fall
You are the one
Who hears my call
When the world's noise
Drowns out my cry
You rescue me
And once more I
Am yours

The day is busy
Bustling, alive
And yet I know not
How I survive
The heat and the anguish
Of the day
Bids me welcome
Yet drives me away

I much prefer
To resume the walking
Listening to
My Saviour talking
I am alive
And I am free
When He is walking
Next to me

Yet, on I go,
once more returning
With a missive
For those yearning
To gain some sense
Of respite
And a chance
To resist the night

For in the darkness
Evil lingers
And in the blackness
Fear doth reign
So grasp the candle
Fearless fingers
And dark will flee
It cannot remain

For the light of Christ
Drives out all fear
And people of light
Ever near
Will greet the day
A brand new morn
As a chance
To be reborn

So, when the world
Seems crazy, battered
And their pain
Was all that mattered
As you wind through
A crowded street
You will in their eyes
Your saviour meet

If you will only
Unveil your eyes
You will see past
Their heavy sighs
And Christ's light
Will once more shine on you
Reflecting God's glory anew

Take forth the rallying Gospel cry
And show the people
Who still sigh
The richness of it's love and hope
And give us all
A chance to hope

Again

The Well at Calvary

When you feel all hope is gone
No reason to go on
When your heart and soul is tired
And you feel uninspired

I love you still

In the realms of deepest fears
Held hostage by unshed tears
Unnamed dread to your heart nears

I'll be there still

Through the sunshine of your joy
Through the rivers of your tears
When people irritate or annoy
In the journey of your years

I'm by your side

When your heart is overflowing
When your soul is filled with knowing
As your spirit is still growing

I'll be there

To guide and refresh you
In wars and in peace
Speaking in soft whispers
Of your heart's release

So when you cry in anguish
And ask where have I gone?
To leave you struggling lonely
And stumble on and on

The truth is, I never left you
I never left your side
I will never forget you
Your paths I'll always guide

So when the fear comes knocking
And the dread's outside your door
Just take a look around you
You'll see I'm there, once more

So, rest and be refreshed child
Sit and drink your fill
And stop and leave your pain there
At the cross, on Calvary's hill

Walk Beside Me:

Take my hand and walk with me awhile
How rarely I see you laugh or smile
Why worry about things that don't last?
Walk beside me, look ahead, forget about the past

I'll be with you today
I'll be with you in all that you say
so trust in Me, and live for now

I ask only for your love
I ask only for your hands
My love for you is wonderful
Stretching over many lands

I'll be with you tomorrow
Together in joy and in sorrow
Hold me forever in your heart
Always together, never apart

Walking With Jesus

Walk with me, I'll show you
Beside me, I'll share
The answers to sorrow
And deepest despair

Take my hand
And follow
Where I will lead
From today
To tomorrow
To my people
In need

And open
The door
To both stranger and friend
My love is in store
A true love, without end

The danger
You fear
Will vanish
For I'm near

Swift as the mist
In the dawn
At the first sign
Of the brand new morn

As swift as the dew
Melts away
When the sun blesses the grass
To start a new day

The anguish you feel
In the depths of your heart
Is desperately real
When we are apart

Let not your heart broken
Be led to despair
With words unspoken
You'll know
How I care

So walk in my shadow
And follow my lead
And take my Good News
To the people
In need

For as you walk with me
And go where I show
The love that you cherish
Will soon start to grow

And words that are spoken
Hearts and minds that are true
Will heal souls that are broken
And offer my love anew

So step out on that road
And share my load
Bringing new dignity
And a chance just to be
With new liberty
In our hearts

For as we go on
And our hearts they are gone
In worship and praise
To the Ancient of Days

We remember the words
And the things we have heard
As we walked by your side
And you were our true guide

Time to pack up the load
And step out on that road
With a spring in our feet
As we go forth and meet
In the eyes of a stranger

Our God

www.ingramcontent.com/pod-product-compliance
Lightning Source LLC
Chambersburg PA
CBHW071733040426
42446CB00012B/2339